Heart To Page

Lauren Huggard

BookLeaf
Publishing

Presentation by *BookLeaf Publishing*

Web: www.bookleafpub.com

E-mail: info@bookleafpub.com

ISBN: 978-93-95755-50-4

First edition 2022

Unexpected pleasantry

I close my eyes expecting terror
instead I receive war, destruction and chaos

I fight to win

the monstrous woman is there
but she's different,
she's kinder than I remember,
she helps me out

Her offer of support takes me aback
Why is she doing this?
We're supposed to be enemies
Where there once was snobbery,
she shows kindness
cleaning up after my mess
keeping her snide comments to herself

When will I wake up to see,
it's not total misery?
Rather,
 just an unexpected pleasantry

Demands of a fur child

tick, tock
goes the clock
time,
rushing away from me,
again!

intentions
to -do lists
friends to meet

it often feels so out of reach
my desires
her desires
my busy schedule
good intentions
poor management

discipline
that's what I need
to turn away
from my news feed

tell her no!
but she cries till I give in
This is the world that I live in
my kitty cat
Ruby
I'm a slave to her every whim!

The hard part is over, dream your dreams

Be gentle on yourself
You've been through enough
Close your eyes and rest your head.

Peace
Be still

Let go
Give everything unto Him,
Who loves you so much
He chose to die for you

An ending and a beginning
Be patient,
You've done the hard stuff

You have power
You have knowledge
You are the expert of your own story

Though you are fearful
You are free

To live life

To follow your dreams
Fly free into the future
And
Dream your Dreams

Yea yea? Yeah.

5

Yea
Yea?
Yeah?

Yeah, yeah, yeah

You just keep saying yeah.

Just....
Yeah.

So if I tell you something
Please don't say
Yeah

Yeah?

It makes me want to pull out my hair,
Do you even care!?

An emotional one

deep
heavy
waves
weight

sadness
inside
how do I contain it?

It's ok to cry
I know that now

I want to cry
need to cry
but the tears won't come out

I open my mouth,
there are the tears
here they are
they come pouring out

softly weeping
I cling to her voice
and
return to my breathing

in and out
slowly
but
surely
returning to myself

here I am
no longer alone

overwhelmed
but not on my own

here I am
I am OK

calm
getting better
returning
            to
                me

If I were a man

I wonder what life would be like,
if I were a man
would I have these worries?

How would I carry my past?
would it be neatly contained?
would it even exist?

would I have these fears?
would I sleep alright at night?
and know I'm safe?

would I have run away?

would I be believed?
would I have the same friends?

would I be ok? If I were a man?
no longer vulnerable,
If I were a man?

not needing anyone to hold my hand

would I stand up tall?
would I be proud?

not needing to be brave , If I were a man

would these scars remain?
what would happen to my pain?

If I were a man,
would I have to explain?
repeat myself ?
over and over again?

life as a man
not afraid of you-
confident,
strong,
would I know what to do?

An ideal life

A loving wife
Most of her life
Devoted
To others
She became a mother

Loving
Gentle
Reliable

No one saw
Her pain inside
All
    that she would hide

Wounds
And pride

As she grew old
It was her personality,
We were told
Quirks
Complaints
Subtle signs of discontent

A child hidden from the adult world
An adult I learnt the truth

How could I not know?
Why didn't they tell me?

We spent hours together
Reading to pass the time
In her tiny room

All that was left of her life,
Memories like trinkets,
squashed into her crystal cabinet
Desires and longings
Not to be met
Her pain
Ever present
In her body
And simmering below the surface

A perfect life
So it seemed
Was it everything she had dreamed?

A devoted wife
He was the love of her life

With him no longer alive
How would she survive?

She took her time
When we thought she'd give up
She held on tight
To see her granddaughter in beautiful white
And when it came night
She closed her eyes so very tight

Breathing her last
She said goodbye
Now she and her love reunite

Young, Healthy and 25

On the outside she seems fine
Young
Healthy
25,
She is alive
She will thrive

"Enjoy it while it lasts "
They say.
Young
Healthy
And 25

But they don't see what's inside.
What's in her heart,
The pain she hides,
She holds it tight
The parts of life
That are filled with strife
How she entered this life

Not young
Not healthy
Not thriving at 25

But she is alive

Her body pushes on
Day by day

On the outside
She seems fine
You wouldn't know what's wrong

No one sees
The organ
Slowly failing her
Lowering each day
Ticking away
Until it gets to zero

Then most people will know
Her illness will start to show

More pills to take
And doctors to see
An operation
For me
living with Chronic Kidney Disease.

Rain

15

Trickling down
It comes with ease
Pouring out of the sky

Wind is gushing
Right by me
The trees are swaying all their leaves

Tiny
I feel
Curled up inside
Under my blankets
 I hide

Safe
Secure
And
Protected

Here I stay
Keeping
The weather at bay

Hope

It comes and it goes
So strong
Inside my mind
Often in my chest I find
There it stays

Hope so strong
So shiny
So new

It helps me
to know what to do

To follow you
Is true hope
Even in times when I want to say nope!
You are my eternal hope
True joy, and love, are found from above

Held by your arms
Seen are all my ways

My future kept safe
by your promises

Family

You love them
You hate them
You don't get to choose them

Some of them are a pain
Some bring joy
Some are complicated
Some you hate

You don't have a choice
You don't get to choose them

Perhaps they choose you
Their biology, their DNA
It's in your veins

Some of them look alike
Some don't

Rumours
Drama
Trauma
And heartache

It's all part of it

It's not something you can fake

Some people run
Some people stay
Some leave
Some are sent away

It's more than a name,
often,
        They're just someone to blame

Sister, oh sister

Oh Sister,
I never really knew how much I missed ya
Until you went and found a mister

It used to be
just you and me

Young
Silly
And
Care free

You taught me a lot
Even when we fought

Inspiring me each day
I never said it
But
I missed you when you went away

How life began to complicate

You there
Me here

Far from reach

Returning to each other
We would talk for hours

About boys and life
and in between,
All the fun that had been

I look back now
And see you there

There's this feeling inside,
Not quite despair
Which I know is not fair

You've grown up
And so have I

But you're still the one I go to when I cry

Always together
When we're apart
I will hold you always in my heart

Inadequacy

Is this right?
Am I doing it right?
Are you sure you want me?
You must be mistaken!

Many a times I've cried
Over and over again,
I've tried
to expel these lies
from my mind

Hiding in plain sight
It's a tough fight!

When I close my eyes at night
I dread the thoughts
                that are sure to come
feeling like
                I
            am
        no one

Fearless woman

A little girl
So frightened of the world
She couldn't see what she would become
Always clinging to her mum
At twelve she still sucked her thumb!

Seventeen she's getting stronger
Frightened of the world no longer
If only she had know then
The way her life would change
in an instant

Dreams so big
She chased them to the end
No reason to hide
or pretend
She found herself some faithful friends
They cheered her on until the end

Eighty five and going grey
"what a wonderful life she had" they will say
Living life day by day
No longer afraid

Wild and free

She saw everything there is to see
Accomplished every dream she dreamed

As I look in the mirror
the face staring back at me,
I wonder,
Will that fearless woman be me?

Gravity of reality

The sun shines in
How she wishes she could feel it on her skin

Working tirelessly
Longing to be free

Staring out the window
The world passes her by

She longs to enjoy
The beauty of the blue skies
She sighs
and rubs her eyes

Back to work
To reality
Pulled back down
By gravity

The weight of responsibility
dull and heavy

Caught in a cycle
that feels so endless

Working hard
trying to spend less

Working hard
day and night
Working hard
until the time is right

Until she can spread her wings
and take flight

Love letter to a bubble buddy

You and me
Together again
Closest of friends

Time well spent
Many days
In lockdown
You turned my frown
Upside down

Eating
Laughing
Joking
Watching the time go by

Seeing you here
All grown up

I smile
Proud of the things
You have done
Still so young
A lot of life to live
And love to give

I thank God for every memory shared
the smile and laughter you bring
Showing me what it is like
 To love our King

There was a horse and the horse was me

There was a horse
And the horse was me

They asked me to choose
one of them,
to put the horse down

it wasn't easy
they weren't direct

they asked me to choose
who would kick me out

"you just don't fit"
"can't you hang out with someone else?"
find new friends is what they meant

a group of girls
teen girls
sometimes mean girls
they stayed in their pack

too afraid to stand up to their leader
they said it was for the best

There was a horse
And the horse was me
they didn't let me down easy
they drowned me, in insecurity.

Control

Holding on tight
I have the illusion of control
Things will turn out right
if I am in control

Two steps forward
it's my turn to roll

Friendships are alright
they don't need to be controlled

Working hard I feel I am in control
Achieving my desired marks,
see!
I have control!

Looking to the past
is that why I need control?
Is that where I lost it?
Where I started
                 to feel out of control?

The future is uncertain,
that, I cannot control
I give it over to my God
 who is sovereign over all.

Open up

Open up
Let them in,
Feel the warmth of their touch
on your skin

Open up
Let me in
I know it's scary,
I know the journey
on which you've been

Open up
Let it go
It's time to set down your load

Open up
So you can see
there is life inside of me

Open up
to those you love
you know they will not judge

Open up
to share the load
you are no longer alone

Habits of endurance

Sometimes she sticks with it,
Sometimes she won't

Sometimes enduring it
for way too long,
Sometimes, not very long at all!

Good things come in time
That's what they say

But how do you know
when it's time to walk away?

When they're not doing their job
do you give them the benefit of the doubt?
And when do you just walk out?

When to be silent?
When to let it all out?

They say opposites attract
But these habits seem so out of whack!

Change in her heart

Six years going strong
She believes she will belong

Looking back on her wrong
Some of it, has been there all along

A word, a song,
A prayer whispered silently,
are her acts of worship

Bringing all glory to Him
Her King

Sometimes it's easy,
her life on the outside
has barely changed

But it's on the inside,
in her heart
where her new life starts

New life
New views
and motivations

no longer striving
not just surviving
but thriving

She is thriving
Like a tree beside water
she has living water in her veins
although it sounds strange
her change
is His name
written on her heart
her new start